Forged in the Mountains

~ ~ ~

A Family's Resilience

A Memoir of Faith, Family, and

the Strength Found in Appalachian Roots

BY

Wilma Gibson Smith

ISBN: 978-1-970435-42-9

Published By: Ink Founders

Dedication

In memory of Eckle and Ruby Gibson

Who forged ten children in the mountains and taught us that faith, family, and love are the only riches worth having.

Eckle and Ruby Gibson

"We are not given a good life or a bad life. We are given a life. It's up to us to make it good or bad."

—Ward Foley

* * *

Contents

Preface

Why I Wrote This Book

I never set out to write a book. For seventy years, I have simply lived my life, raised a family, taught school, played music, and tended cattle. The stories I tell in these pages are not ones I thought anyone else would care to hear; they are simply my memories, the moments that shaped me, and the people who made me who I am.

But something happened when I turned seventy. I looked at my grandchildren and realized they were growing up in a world so different from the one I knew. They have never gone to bed hungry. They have never had to wear socks on their hands because gloves were too expensive. They have never watched a father come home from the coal mines with hands so stained that no amount of scrubbing could clean them.

And I thought: *How will they know?* How will they understand where they come from, what their great-grandparents sacrificed, or the values their family was built upon?

This book is my answer to those questions. It is a record of a way of life that is disappearing, a testimony to people who will never be famous but who deserve to be remembered. I wrote this for my grandchildren, so they will know the coal miner and his wife who gave everything so their children could have a better life. It is for my siblings, so we can remember together the lessons Mama and Daddy taught us. And it is for anyone who has ever wondered if they can overcome their circumstances or felt that where they come from determines where they can go.

I wrote this book because these stories matter. The small moments—Daddy's garden, Mama's washing machine, the music we made together, the hand-me-down dresses—these are the threads that weave a life. When you pull those threads together, a pattern emerges: one of faith, family, love, and perseverance.

These are not just my values. They are the values of countless families who built this country; families who raised children in poverty and taught them that true wealth has nothing to do with money. If this book helps even one person understand that truth, then every hour I spent writing it was worth it.

This is not a story of fame or fortune. It is a story of ordinary people who did extraordinary things simply by showing up every day, loving fiercely, working honestly, and never giving up. It is the story of how coal dust can become gold when refined by faith and love.

These are my memories. This is my testimony. This is my gift to those who come after.

"Tell it to your children, and let your children tell it to their children, and their children to the next generation."

— Joel 1:3

Acknowledgments

This book would not exist without the countless people who have shaped my life and supported this journey of remembrance.

First and foremost, I thank my parents, Eckle and Ruby Gibson. Everything good in me came from you. Daddy, your coal-stained hands built more than you ever knew. Mama, your endless love fed more than our bodies. You taught me that true wealth cannot be measured in dollars, only in faith, family, and love.

To my nine siblings: Herschel (whom we lost too soon), Minnie Pearl, Hubert, Freda, Doug, Dorothy, Brenda, Harriet, and Clarence, we were forged together in those mountains. You are my first friends, and our bond as Gibson children will never break.

To my first husband of forty-four years, thank you for the life we built. To my current husband, thank you for the music and for supporting my need to write. To my son and grandchildren: you are the reason I wrote this book. I want you to know where you come from, to understand the sacrifices that were made, to carry forward the values that your great-grandparents lived by. You are part of a legacy that stretches back through generations of strong, faithful, hardworking people. Never forget that.

And finally, to God, who carried me through every valley and reached for me when I was drowning in grief. This book is a testimony to Your faithfulness.

To my readers: Thank you for walking through the mountains with me. May you find something here that speaks to your own journey.

Prologue

The Call to Remember

It was a cold February morning when I stood in my kitchen in Lawrenceburg, Tennessee, looking out at the cattle grazing in the field. My husband was already out tending to the new calves, and I had the house to myself; a rare moment of quiet in our busy life on the farm.

I poured myself a cup of coffee and sat down at the kitchen table. As I sat there, I thought about another kitchen table years ago in Lee County, Virginia, where I taught school and where my son was raised. It was at that table that I graded papers after long days in the classroom, where my son spread out his homework, and where we shared simple meals and conversations that shaped our lives. And suddenly, without warning, a memory came to me so vivid it took my breath away.

I was seven years old again, standing in my father's garden in Kemmergem, Virginia. I could feel the rich mountain soil between my fingers, see Daddy's coal-stained hands gently placing seeds in the furrows he had made, hear his voice telling me about making promises and keeping them.

"You put these in the ground," he had said, "and you are making a promise."

Sitting there in my Tennessee kitchen, seventy years later, I realized that my entire life has been about keeping promises. The promise to tend what has been planted. The promise to honor where I came from. The promise to pass on the lessons my parents taught me.

And I realized something else: I was the last one who could tell these stories the way they needed to be told. My siblings and I are scattered now; some are already gone. My parents have been at rest for years. The world that built me, a world of coal mines and hand-me-downs, of Saturday night music and neighbors who shared everything they had—that world is disappearing.

If I do not write it down, who will remember? If I do not tell the truth about what poverty felt like, the faith that sustained us, and how love can fill a house that has nothing else—who will know?

This is not an easy story to tell. There are parts that still make me cry and memories that bring back the ache of loss. There are moments I would rather forget: the hunger, the grief, and the feeling of being orphaned, even when I was grown with children of my own.

But these stories are not mine to keep. They belong to my children and grandchildren. They belong to anyone who has ever struggled and wondered if they would make it. They belong to every person who needs to hear that where you start does not determine where you finish, that poverty of circumstances does not mean poverty of spirit.

So, I sat down and began to write. I wrote about Daddy's hands and Mama's washing machine. I wrote about ten Gibson children growing up in a house filled with love, noise, and music. I wrote about loss and grief and the voice of God saying, *"It's enough."* I wrote about the hard parts and the beautiful parts, the despair and the grace.

The story you are about to read is true. These are my memories, my family, my life. I have tried to tell it honestly, without pretending poverty was somehow noble or that struggle was easy. But I want to show you what was gained in the midst of all that was lacked.

My parents forged ten children in the mountains of Appalachia. They gave us very little money, but they gave us a wealth of love, faith, and values.

This is their story. This is our story. This is my gift to you.

Now come with me. Let me take you to a small house in Kemmergem, Virginia, where a coal miner and his wife are raising ten children and teaching them that true wealth cannot be measured in dollars. Let me show you what it means to be forged in the mountains.

Let me show you how coal dust becomes gold.

"Remember the days of old; consider the generations long past. Ask your father, and he will tell you; your elders, and they will explain it to you."
*— **Deuteronomy 32:7***

PART ONE

Roots and Foundation

"A cord of three strands is not quickly broken."

—Ecclesiastes 4:12

Chapter 1

Roots in the Mountains

I was born in 1956 in the Appalachian Mountains of Virginia, a place most people have never heard of, but one that shaped everything I would become. My earliest memories are of Kemmergem, where I grew up surrounded by rolling hills and the constant presence of family. We were ten children in all, and our small home was filled with noise, laughter, and love that made up for everything we lacked in material wealth.

My father was a coal miner, like so many men in our community. Every morning before dawn, he would leave for the mines, lunch pail in hand and determination in his step. He hardly ever missed a day of work, no matter how exhausted he was or how much his body ached. That dedication taught me more about responsibility and perseverance than any textbook ever could.

I can still see my father's hands; coal dust embedded so deep in the creases that no amount of scrubbing could lift it. They were rough, calloused, and permanently stained. As a child, I thought everyone's daddy had hands like that.

One evening, when I was about seven, I watched him wash up at the pump outside. He scrubbed and scrubbed with harsh lye soap, and I asked him why the black would not come out. He looked at his hands for a long moment, then looked at me and said, *"This is honest dirt, Wilma. It's the price of taking care of my family, and I wear it with pride."*

I didn't fully understand then, but those words stayed with me. Years later, when I was struggling through college, working multiple jobs, and wondering if I could make it, I would think of those coal-stained hands and find the strength to keep going.

My mother was the heart of our home. Without modern conveniences, she raised ten children with nothing but an old-fashioned washing machine and endless determination. I can still see her at that machine, her hands working tirelessly to keep us clean. Our old-fashioned cookstove filled the house with warmth and the scent of dinner, and in the winter, we gathered around the fireplace for heat. We were poor by any standard measure, but we were rich in the things that truly mattered.

Behind our house, Daddy kept a vegetable garden. This wasn't a hobby—it was survival. That garden meant the difference between eating and going hungry. He would work the soil after his shift at the mine, even when his body was spent, and his back was screaming at him to rest.

I was about ten when Daddy taught me how to plant. He showed me how to draw the rows, how deep to nestle each seed, and how to mound the soil around the base of the tomato plants. His coal-blackened hands, usually so rugged, were so gentle with those tiny seeds.

"When you put these in the ground, Wilma," he told me, "you are making a promise. A promise to tend them, water them, and care for them. If you keep your promise, they will keep theirs—they will feed you."

One summer, I was responsible for the beans. Every day, I'd check their progress, pulling weeds and watching for bugs. When those first beans came in, and Mama cooked them for supper, Daddy made a big show of how good they were. "Best beans I ever tasted," he said. In that moment, I felt ten feet tall.

Years later, when I had my own students, I often thought about those beans. I realized then that teaching is much like gardening: you plant seeds, you tend them with care, and if you are patient and faithful, you eventually get to see them grow.

Family Beyond Our Walls

Growing up in Kemmergem, we weren't just surrounded by our immediate family of twelve; we had extended family all around us, woven into the fabric of our daily lives.

My paternal grandparents, Arlin and Minnie Gibson, lived within walking distance. My maternal grandparents, Harrison and Elizabeth Collins, were only about a mile away. Even two of my father's sisters, Aunt Maude and Aunt Frankie, lived just a short walking distance from our home.

I really enjoyed spending time with both sets of grandparents because they had wisdom to share. There is something special about the bond with a grandparent; they have the time and patience that parents—busy with the exhausting work of keeping ten children fed and clothed—sometimes cannot afford. Our grandparents had lived through tough times, raised their own children through poverty; they carried lessons to pass on that only a lifetime of struggle and survival can teach.

Between Aunt Maude and Aunt Frankie, we had eleven first cousins. Because their ages matched mine and my siblings', almost one-to-one with our family, we always had playmates, always had someone our own age to run with.

We cousins played together constantly. We played games of dolls and dress-up, or played tag until we were breathless and exhausted. We swung on wild grapevines, feeling like we were flying through the forest, and turned the mountains and hollows around us into a magical kingdom of our own making. Whatever came to mind, we played it. With that many kids around the same ages, there was never a shortage of imagination or fun.

It was great growing up with an extended family close by. When I look back now, I realize how rare and precious that closeness was. We were not just a family of twelve living in isolation; we were part of a vast, protective network of Gibsons and Collinses who all looked out for one another. If Mama needed something, Aunt Maude or Aunt Frankie was just a short walk away. If we kids needed a watchful eye, there were grandparents nearby. If someone had extra from their garden, it was shared around.

That sense of belonging to something bigger than our own household shaped the people we became. We learned early on that family isn't just the people under your roof—it's the people who show up, who share, who play with your children, and pass their wisdom down to the next generation.

Underpinning all of this was a deep-rooted sense of spirit. Our parents instilled in us a strong Christian faith and a moral foundation intended to guide us through whatever life brought our way. They taught us to be honest, to work hard, and to love one another fiercely.

These weren't just words to them; they lived these values every single day.

"For every house is built by someone, but God is the builder of everything."
— Hebrews 3:4

Chapter 2

The Day Everything Changed

I was only six years old when tragedy struck our family. My oldest brother, just twenty-three, was killed in a car accident. I had never seen death up close before, and I had certainly never seen my parents—those pillars of strength—break down the way they did.

It terrified me. The grief that filled our house was thick and heavy, a weight I didn't yet understand. My parents, who had always been so strong, were suddenly vulnerable and broken. But even in their deepest pain, they showed us something important: they showed us how to grieve, how to lean on faith, and how to eventually find the strength to keep going.

That loss left a mark on all of us, but it also taught me about the fragility of life and the importance of cherishing every moment with the people you love.

"The Lord is close to the brokenhearted and saves those who are crushed in spirit."
— **Psalm 34:18**

Chapter 3

Growing Up with Purpose

Despite our poverty, I was an outgoing, friendly child. I made friends easily and found joy in simple things. My formative years were spent watching my parents work themselves to the bone, and their example became the blueprint for my own life.

I saw how my mother managed a household without any of the modern conveniences other families took for granted. I watched my father leave for the dangerous work of the coal mines day after day, never complaining, always providing. Their work ethic, their integrity, and their unwavering commitment to family became the foundation of who I would become.

School was a place where I thrived socially, though the path wasn't always smooth. Life eventually took a turn, and I dropped out in the eleventh grade. At the time, it felt like a defeat, as if I had let both myself and my parents down. But giving up was never how I was raised.

I eventually obtained my GED, proving to myself that I could finish what I started. But I didn't stop there. I went on to a four-year college and earned my teaching degree. That girl from a coal-mining family, who grew up with an old-fashioned washing machine and a wood-burning stove, became a teacher. It was living proof that where you come from does not determine where you are going.

"Commit to the Lord whatever you do, and he will establish your plans."
— Proverbs 16:3

Chapter 4

Ten Strong — Growing Up Gibson

Being the youngest of ten children meant I was never alone and never without someone looking out for me. My brothers and sisters were my first friends, protectors, playmates, and my teachers. We were a unit, bound together not just by blood, but by the shared experience of growing up in the mountains of Kemmergem.

Even after my oldest brother passed away, there were still nine of us; a houseful of big personalities, big dreams, and plenty of noise. We learned early on that we had to stick together; family was everything when you didn't have much else.

Music in Our Blood

If there was one thing that truly united us, it was music. All but two of my siblings learned to play the guitar, and our home was constantly filled with the sound of strumming strings and blending voices. On weekends, it was common for us to gather with neighbors. Someone would pull out a guitar, and before long, we would have a full-on jam session.

These were not performances; they were gatherings. Mr. Henderson from down the road would bring his fiddle, and the Johnsons would come over with their children. We would push the furniture back in our small living room to make a dance floor, and the music would flow: gospel hymns, old mountain songs, and country tunes we all knew by heart. In those days, there were no strangers in Kemmergem, just extended family who did not happen to share our last name.

Winter Games and Summer Adventures

In the winter, we went sledding down the hills wearing old socks on our hands because real gloves were a luxury we could not afford. Those socks would get soaking wet and freeze stiff until our hands turned red with cold, but we did not care. We were flying down those hills, laughing and screaming, alive with pure joy.

We spent our summers wrestling, playing hide-and-seek in the woods, and building forts out of whatever we could find. Sometimes, the wrestling got too rough. Things would get out of hand, and play would turn into real anger. When Daddy saw a fight brewing, he had a unique way of handling it: he would make the two of us stand and hug each other until the anger melted away. It sounds simple, even silly, but it worked. It is hard to stay mad at someone when you are forced to embrace them, when you can feel their heart beating and remember they are your brother or sister. That was another way he taught us to love one another.

Being the youngest, I always wanted to do exactly what my older siblings did, even when it wasn't a good idea. I remember the time we wanted to swing on a grapevine, but a small tree stood in the way. The older kids chopped it down, leaving a three-foot-tall stump that was jagged and pointed at the top.

When it was my turn, I swung out as far as I could. As I came back toward the others standing on the bank, I didn't come back far enough for them to catch me. I held on tightly to that grapevine until my strength gave out and I had to let go. I fell, landing straddled across that pointed stump. If I had been impaled on it, I would not be here today.

Another thing we did for fun was roll tires down a steep hill. Some of us would stand at the top and send them racing downward, while those at the bottom would try to catch them by sticking their arms through them. Not wanting to feel left out or to be told I was too little, I asked if I could catch one.

I stood at the bottom of the hill with my arms stretched wide, ready and determined. Someone rolled a tire down. The tire came down so fast it bounced right as it reached me, hitting me straight in the face and knocking me down. My face went numb instantly. My older siblings rushed over and carried me back to the house. Thankfully, I wasn't seriously injured.

The Sisterhood of Hand-Me-Downs

Having five sisters meant one thing for certain: you didn't get new clothes. You wore hand-me-downs, clothes that older sisters had outgrown. As the youngest, I was at the end of a long line of inheritance.

And that was okay. By the time a dress got to me, it had been worn, washed, and mended, but it was new to me. I'd see my sister's dress and dream about the day it would finally be mine. When that day came, I wore it with pride because it connected me to my sisters, to their stories, and the lives those dresses had lived before they reached me.

We understood that our parents were struggling, but we never let them know we knew. We saw Mama staying up late to mend those clothes so they would last for another daughter; we saw Daddy working extra shifts when someone needed shoes. We knew they were doing the best they could and appreciated it, but we pretended we didn't know their struggles because we understood that our parents were giving us everything they had.

Finding My Voice

While most of us learned the guitar, I was the only one who took a serious interest in music as more than just a pastime. Music spoke to something deep in my soul. When I played and sang, I felt free in a way I couldn't quite explain.

At the age of twelve, I had my first country and western band. Imagine that: a twelve-year-old girl from the mountains of Virginia with her own band! We entertained at various venues and actually got paid for it. It was not much, but it was enough to contribute to the family and feel like I was doing my part.

Music became my passion and, for a time, my identity. Up until my thirties, I led two other bands. Almost every weekend, we were hired for church socials, community gatherings, or small venues in neighboring towns. The music that had started around our family fireplace eventually carried me out into the world. I even recorded a record with my last band. When I held that vinyl in my hands for the first time, with my name printed on it, I thought about all those jam sessions in our tiny living room, my siblings and neighbors crowded together, making music simply for the joy of it. That record was proof that the girl from Kemmergem, the youngest of ten, the one who wore hand-me-downs and socks for gloves, could make something that would last.

The Lessons of Being Ten

Growing up as one of ten taught me things I could not have learned any other way. I learned to share, not because it was noble, but because it was necessary. I learned to find joy in simple things because simple things were all we had. I learned that love does not require fancy gifts; love is standing in an embrace with your brother until the anger melts away.

I learned that "new" does not always mean better, and that a hand-me-down dress carries the warmth of the sisters who wore it before you. I learned that music can feed your soul when your stomach is not quite full. Most importantly, I learned that community is not just the people who live near you; it is the people who show up, who share, and who help you through the tough times.

My siblings and I are scattered now, our lives having taken us in different directions. But we carry Kemmergem with us. We carry the lessons from Mama and Daddy. We carry the memory of ten Gibson children who did not have much, yet had everything that truly mattered.

We were ten strong, and that strength has carried each of us through whatever life has brought our way.

"Behold, how good and pleasant it is when brothers dwell in unity!"

— Psalm 133:1

PART TWO

Love, Loss, And Redemption

"The Lord is close to the brokenhearted and saves those who are crushed in spirit."

—Psalm 34:18

Chapter 5

Building a Life Together

I married my first husband, and together we built a life that would span forty-four years. Much like my parents before me, we faced our share of financial challenges. There were seasons when money was tight, and the future felt uncertain, but we faced every obstacle together, just as I had learned from watching my parents weather their own storms.

Our marriage was built on the same foundation my parents had given me: faith, hard work, and an unshakeable commitment. We supported each other through the lean times and celebrated the good ones. For over four decades, we were partners in every sense of the word.

When he passed away, it felt like losing a part of my own soul. But by then, I had already learned that while grief could bend me, the foundation my parents built would never let me break.

"Two are better than one... if either of them falls down, one can help the other up."

— **Ecclesiastes 4:9-10**

Chapter 6

When the Pillars Fall

There are moments in life that divide everything into "before" and "after." For our family, those moments came with the loss of our parents; first Mama, and then, fifteen years later, Daddy. These were more than just deaths; they represented the crumbling of the foundation upon which we had built our entire lives.

Mama's Long Goodbye

Our mother was the first to leave us. She suffered a severe heart attack, and for a moment, we thought we had lost her then and there. But with God's help, she lived another five years. Those were precious years, borrowed time that we cherished, even as we watched her grow more fragile.

After those five years, her health began to decline again, and she deteriorated quickly. One day, she was managing; the next, she was in the hospital, and we all knew in our hearts that this time was different.

The entire family stayed at the hospital to be with her. All ten of us children, grown now with families of our own, gathered around our mother. The hospital staff tried to persuade us to go home and rest, but we could not leave. She had never left us, not once in our entire lives, and we were not going to leave her now.

One rainy morning, she began to slip away. The depth of our grief is impossible to explain; it was a collective breaking, ten hearts shattering at once. We held her hands, told her we loved her, and thanked her for everything she had given us. And then, she was gone.

The woman who had scrubbed our clothes on that old washing machine, who had cooked over a wood stove, who had stretched every dollar and every meal to feed ten children, and who had loved us with a fierceness that made up for everything we lacked—she was gone.

Daddy's Broken Heart

Having our father still with us helped, but it was so hard to see his heartbreak, while we were dealing with our own grief. Daddy had loved Mama with everything he had for all those years. They had been partners through poverty, through the loss of their oldest son, and through the grueling work of raising ten children on a coal miner's wages. She had been his other half.

After Mama passed, something went out of Daddy. He kept going, because that is what he did, but the light in his eyes had dimmed. He still attended family gatherings, told his stories, and showed up for his children and grandchildren, but we could see the loneliness in him. We saw it in the way he looked at Mama's empty chair and heard it in the way his voice caught whenever he mentioned her name.

For fifteen years, Daddy lived without his beloved Ruby. Fifteen years of carrying on, of being strong for us, and of missing the woman who had been by his side through everything.

Christmas Day

Daddy was eighty-nine years old when he fell and broke his hip. At his age, we knew it was serious, but Daddy had always been strong. He had worked in the coal mines for decades; surely, we thought, he could recover from this.

But the injury spiraled into a nightmare we could never have imagined. He developed one infection after another. Each time the doctors gained control, a new one would flare up. We watched him weaken and struggle, helpless to do anything but remain by his side and pray.

Early on Christmas Day, Daddy left us to be with Mama.

The cruelty of the timing was lost on no one. Christmas—a day of celebration, of family gathered together in joy and light—became the day we lost our father. For us, the holiday would never be the same.

Orphans

In that moment, we felt like orphans. It does not matter if you are a grown adult with children and grandchildren of your own; when your parents die, you become an orphan. Our parents had been the pillars of our entire lives. They were always there; through every challenge, every triumph, every moment of doubt or fear. They were our anchor, our compass, and our safe harbor. Suddenly, we did not know how to live without them.

The world felt unmoored. Who would we call for advice? Who would hold the family together for Christmas and Thanksgiving? Who would tell the old stories, reminding us of our roots in Kemmergem? When Mama died, we still had Daddy. When Daddy died, we had each other, but the generation that came before us, the one that had survived the Great Depression, raised ten children in poverty, and worked themselves to the bone to give us a better life, that generation was gone.

The Darkness

After Daddy's passing, I got stuck in my grief. It was not just sadness; it was something darker and deeper. For more than three years, I was severely depressed, going through the motions of living without really living at all.

I woke up each morning feeling the crushing weight of his absence. When Christmas returned, instead of celebration, I could only see that rainy hospital room and hear Daddy's last breath. I felt like an orphan at an age when I should have been celebrating retirement and grandchildren.

I stopped finding joy in the things I used to love. Music no longer moved me the way it once had. Family gatherings felt hollow without Mama and Daddy's presence. I smiled when I was supposed to smile, laughed when something was supposed to be funny, but inside, I was drowning in a grief so deep I could not see the surface.

My family tried to help. My siblings, who were dealing with their own grief, reached out. My husband held me when I cried. But I was trapped in that dark valley, unable to find my way out. The world continued around me, but I felt disconnected from all of it, like I was watching life happen behind thick glass.

"It's Enough"

Then, after three years of this weight, something miraculous happened. God touched me. I heard Him say, quite clearly: *"It's enough."*

I was sitting in my living room, the same depression weighing on me like it had for three years, when those words reached me. It wasn't necessarily an audible voice, but it was unmistakable. God was telling me that the season of this grief was over.

It felt as if a physical weight had been lifted, as if I had been permitted to live again. This wasn't a command to forget Daddy—I could never forget—but to honor his memory by living the way he taught me: to face the day with determination, to love my family fiercely, and to keep my faith.

From that point on, I was able to move forward. The grief did not disappear entirely; you never stop missing your parents, but it transformed into something I could carry, rather than something that was drowning me.

Their Legacy Lives On

Looking back now, I understand that losing our parents is a part of the "cruel mathematics" of life. It is the natural order of things, yet understanding that truth never makes the reality any easier to bear.

What I have learned, however, is that they are not really gone. Mama lives on every time I show kindness to someone who is struggling, every time I "make do" with what I have, and every time I put my family first. Daddy lives on every time I persevere through difficulty, every time I take pride in honest work, and every time I teach others that integrity matters more than comfort.

Their values, their faith, and their love did not die with them. These things live on in me, in my siblings, and in our children and grandchildren. The pillars may have fallen, but the foundation they built remains.

We are Gibson children, raised in the mountains of Kemmergem by a coal miner and his devoted wife. That truth shapes us, guides us, and sustains us still.

Mama and Daddy are together now, reunited after fifteen years apart. I know that one day, when my own time comes, I will see them again. Until then, I carry them with me; in my memories, in my choices, and in the very fabric of who I am.

That spiritual transformation reminded me that faith isn't just something you hold onto during the good times; it is what carries you through the valley when you can no longer carry yourself. And sometimes, when you have been in that valley long enough, God Himself reaches down and says, "It is enough. It is time to live again."

"He heals the brokenhearted and binds up their wounds."

— **Psalm 147:3**

PART THREE

Reflection and Legacy

"The fruit of the righteous is a tree of life, and whoever captures souls is wise."

—Proverbs 11:30

Chapter 7

The Threads That Bind

Looking back over seventy years of life, I can clearly see the threads that have woven their way through everything: family, faith, and love.

Family has always been my anchor. From those early days in *Kemmergem* with my nine siblings, to my own marriage and the family we built together, to the extended family that continues to grow, family has been everything. We may not have had much in terms of material wealth, but we had each other, and that was always more than enough.

Faith has been my compass. The Christian values my parents instilled in me as a child have guided every decision, every challenge, and every triumph. When I was lost in the depths of grief, it was faith that eventually led me back to the light. When times were hard, it was faith that reminded me I was never alone.

Love has been the fuel. It was the love my parents showed us, even when they had so little to give materially. It was the love I shared with my husband for forty-four years. It was the love that kept me going when I didn't think I could take another step. Love is what makes everything else possible.

"And now these three remain: faith, hope, and love. But the greatest of these is love."
— 1 Corinthians 13:13

Chapter 8

Ten Paths from One Home

We started in the same place: a small house in Kemmergem, Virginia, with parents who worked themselves to the bone to keep us fed and clothed. We shared hand-me-down clothes, wore socks for gloves, and learned to play music together on weekend evenings. We were the Gibson children, and we were ten strong.

But life took each of us in different directions. Some of us stayed close to home, while others traveled the world. Some followed traditional paths, while others forged new ones. Each of us carried the lessons Mama and Daddy taught us, applying them in our own unique ways.

The Paths We Took

Herschel: The One We Lost Too Soon

Herschel was the oldest, the firstborn, who paved the way for the rest of us. He married and had a beautiful daughter, eventually settling in Rockwood, Maryland, to build a life for his young family.

But when his daughter was only three years old, tragedy struck. Herschel was killed in a car accident at just twenty-three. I was only six when it happened, and I still remember the grief that shattered our home. He was taken far too soon, before he could see his daughter grow up, and before he could fulfill the dreams he held. Herschel's death taught us that life is precious and fragile, and that tomorrow is never guaranteed. His memory remains a reminder to cherish every moment and every person we love.

Minnie Pearl: The Sister Who Stayed Close

Minnie Pearl married and had three sons, making her home in Jonesville, Virginia, not far from where we grew up. She stayed connected to her roots, to the mountains that shaped us, and to the community that raised us.

She lived her entire life in Jonesville, raising her boys and remaining the heart of our family gatherings. Minnie Pearl has since passed away, but her legacy lives on in her sons and in the memories of those Sunday dinners where her laughter filled the room.

Hubert: The Soldier Who Came Home

Hubert served his country in the Army for four years. When his service ended, he returned to Kemmergem, the place that would always be home. He married and had two sons and a daughter, building his life in the same mountains where he was raised.

Hubert understood something important: sometimes the best place to build a life is exactly where your roots are. Though he is gone now, he lived his life close to family, close to the values we were raised with, and close to everything that mattered most

Freda: The Housewife Who Ventured North

Freda married and moved to North Baltimore, Ohio, farther from home than most of us ventured. She became a homemaker, devoting herself entirely to raising her two sons and her daughter.

While she lived far from the Virginia mountains, she carried them with her in the way she managed her household and nurtured her children. Freda has passed on now, but she proved that you can take the girl out of the mountains, but you cannot take the mountains out of the girl. No matter where we go, we carry Mama and Daddy's lessons with us.

Doug: The Airman Who Served

Doug married and spent four years in the Air Force, serving his country just as Hubert had done. After the Air Force, Doug went to work for the Postal Service in Roanoke, Virginia, where he currently lives. He had two sons and one daughter.

Doug found his calling in service—first to his nation, then to his community. He remains in Virginia, still deeply connected to the region that shaped us all.

Dorothy: The Healer

Dorothy became a Licensed Practical Nurse, spending most of her career in Indiana. She had three sons and devoted her life to the care of others. Dorothy took Mama's natural gift for nurturing and turned it into a profession, spending her days healing those in need. Though she has passed away, her legacy lives on through the countless patients she helped. She showed us that the compassion we learned at home could change lives far beyond our family.

Brenda: The Entrepreneur

Brenda lives in Woodway, Virginia, and owns her own business. As a mother of two daughters, she proved that a girl from the mountains could become a successful businesswoman. Brenda took the work ethic Daddy taught us in his garden and the coal mines and built something of her own. She is still running her business today, still living close to where we grew up, still showing everyone that determination and hard work can create opportunities even when you start with nothing.

Harriet: The Caregiver Who Never Quit

Harriet moved to Woodway, Virginia, and obtained her CNA license. She continues that work today, caring for those who need help. Even while raising two sons and a daughter, she never stopped working to serve others. Harriet is still at it—embodying the perseverance Mama and Daddy modeled for us. While some choose to retire, Harriet keeps going because helping people is simply who she is.

Clarence: The Airman Who Saw the World

Clarence entered the Air Force after marrying and was stationed in England and Guam. Imagine that: a boy from Kemmergem, Virginia, seeing the world and living in countries most of us had only read about in books. After the Air Force, he went to work for Lockheed Martin, where he eventually retired. The father of three daughters, Clarence's journey took him the farthest from home, but showed us that the sky truly is the limit; the lessons he learned in that small house in the mountains carried him around the world and into a successful career.

Wilma: The Teacher Who Never Stopped Learning

And then there is me, the youngest of the ten. My path took me from dropping out in the eleventh grade to earning my GED and finally to completing my college degree. I spent thirty-three years teaching Language Arts to seventh and eighth graders.

I had one son. Today, I live in Lawrenceburg, Tennessee, where my husband and I cattle farm.

I took the lessons Daddy taught me in his garden, about planting seeds and tending them faithfully, and applied them to the classroom. Now, in my retirement, as I watch new calves come into the world, I am reminded that new beginnings are always possible.

What It All Means

Look at us; ten children from one poor family in the Appalachian Mountains. A soldier, an airman, nurses, a teacher, a businesswoman, a postal worker, parents, and caregivers. Some of us stayed close to home, while others traveled the world. Some are still here, and others have passed on. But every single one of us made something of our lives.

We didn't all become rich, and we didn't all become famous. But we all became *something*: people of integrity, people who worked hard, people who loved our families, and people who contributed to our communities. We became exactly what Mama and Daddy raised us to be.

This should tell you something important: no matter what background you come from, you can be anything you want to be. Ten children, one small house, and parents who worked in coal mines and washed clothes on an old-fashioned machine, and look at what became of us

We are proof that where you start doesn't determine where you finish. We are proof that poverty of circumstance doesn't mean poverty of spirit. We are proof that love, faith, and determination can overcome any obstacle. We were ten strong then, and those of us who remain are still strong now. We carry Mama and Daddy with us in everything we do, in every choice we make, in every value we hold dear.

Ten paths from one home, and every single path led somewhere worth going.

"There are different kinds of gifts, but the same Spirit distributes them."
— 1 Corinthians 12:4

Chapter 9

Lessons for the Journey

The lessons I learned growing up poor in Appalachia, watching my father labor in the coal mines and my mother pour her soul into our home, have remained the steady heartbeat of my life.

I learned that I could be anything I wanted to be. That eleventh-grade dropout who went on to earn a college degree and become a teacher is proof that your circumstances do not define your potential. Your beginning does not have to dictate your end.

I learned to always be honest with people. My parents taught me that integrity is non-negotiable. It is the one thing no one can take from you, and I have carried that truth through every relationship and every challenge.

Most importantly, I learned to remain faithful to God, especially when the path grows dark. When my father passed away on Christmas Day and I fell into that deep, suffocating depression, my faith may have wavered, but it never broke. When God finally spoke to me after those three long years, I was reminded of the greatest truth of all: He had never once left my side.

"The path of the righteous is like the morning sun, shining ever brighter till the full light of day."
— **Proverbs 4:18**

Chapter 10

Words for Those Who Come After

If there is one thing I want people to understand from my story, it is this: it doesn't matter where you come from or how little you have. You can accomplish anything you set your mind to. I am living proof of that truth.

Life will be hard sometimes; there is no avoiding it. You will face losses that break your heart, financial struggles, and obstacles that seem impossible to overcome. But with prayer and patience, you will navigate those seasons. I promise you that.

Most importantly, remember that nothing and no one is worth changing yourself for just to be accepted. The values my parents taught me, the faith they instilled in me, and the person they raised me to be were never up for negotiation. Stay true to who you are.

I am seventy years old now, and I have lived most of my life in Pennington Gap, Virginia, not far from where I grew up. I have watched the world change in ways my parents could never have imagined, but the fundamental truths they taught me remain unchanged:

Work hard. Love fiercely. Keep the faith. Stay honest. Never give up.

These simple lessons from a coal miner's daughter have carried me through every season of life, and they will carry you, too. This is my story—not of fame or fortune, but of family, faith, and the quiet perseverance that turns struggles into strength and coal dust into gold.

"One generation commends your works to another; they tell of your mighty acts."
— **Psalm 145:4**

Epilogue

Looking Forward

As I sit here on my cattle farm in Tennessee, seventy years old and still discovering what life has to teach me, I think about beginnings and endings, about seeds and harvests, about the promises we make and the promises we keep.

Every spring, I watch new calves being born. Every spring, I am reminded that new life is always possible, that no matter how harsh the winter, growth returns. This is what my father taught me in that garden so long ago, and it is what I have tried to live by ever since.

The mountains of Kemmergem are far from here now, but I carry them with me. I carry Mama's determination and Daddy's work ethic. I carry the memory of ten Gibson children learning to love fiercely and forgive quickly. I carry the music we made together, the meals we shared, the faith that sustained us.

My grandchildren will never know poverty the way I knew it. They will never wear socks for gloves or wonder if there will be enough food. And I am grateful for that. But I hope they know something even more important: that true wealth has nothing to do with money.

I hope they know that a coal miner with stained hands can build a fortune in family and faith. I hope they know that dropping out of school is not the end of education, that setbacks are not failures, that where you come from gives you strength for where you are going.

I hope they read this book and understand that they come from a strong stock. That they are descendants of people who faced poverty and grief and loss with dignity and grace. That their legacy is not one of wealth or fame, but of integrity, perseverance, and love.

As for me, I am still teaching; no longer in a classroom, but in the way I live. I am still planting seeds and tending them. I am still making music. I am still believing that God has plans for me, that each day is a gift, and that it is never too late for new beginnings.

The mountains forged me. Faith sustained me. Family defined me. And love, the love that filled a small house in Kemmergem despite all we lacked, that love continues to be the greatest wealth I have ever known.

This is my testimony. This is my gift. This is my promise kept.

May you find your own mountains to climb, your own gardens to tend, your own promises to keep. And may you discover, as I have, that the greatest fortunes are those that cannot be counted, only felt and shared and passed on to the next generation.

The story continues. The legacy lives on. The seeds are still growing.

Thank you for walking through the mountains with me.

"See, I am doing a new thing! Now it springs up; do you not perceive it?"
— **Isaiah 43:19**

Afterword

A Note to Readers

Thank you for reading my story. If you have made it this far, you have walked with me through seventy years of memories, through the mountains of Virginia and the valleys of grief, through the joys of family and the triumph of perseverance.

I want you to know that every word is true. These are not embellished tales or idealized memories. This is what happened. This is how we lived. These are the people who shaped me.

Most importantly, I hope you will take the lessons I learned and make them your own. Plant your seeds. Tend them faithfully. Love fiercely. Keep your promises. Stay true to your values. Have faith.

And remember: you can accomplish anything you set your mind to, no matter where you come from.

With love and gratitude,

Wilma Gibson Goins Smith

Lawrenceburg, Tennessee

The Gibson Family Tree

Eckle Gibson m. Ruby Collins

1. Herschel (1940-1963) married – 1 daughter

2. Minnie Pearl (deceased) married – 3 sons

3. Hubert (deceased) married – 2 sons, 1 daughter

4. Freda (deceased) married – 2 sons, 1 daughter

5. Doug, married – 2 sons, 1 daughter

6. Dorothy (deceased) married – 3 sons

7. Brenda, married – 2 daughters

8. Harriet, married – 2 sons, 2 daughters

9. Clarence, married – 3 daughters

10. Wilma, married – 1 son, 2 grandchildren

Timeline of Key Events

1920s: Eckle Gibson and Ruby Collins born

1940: Herschel Gibson born (eldest child)

1940s-1950s: Nine more Gibson children born

1956: Wilma Gibson·born (youngest of ten children), Kemmergem, Virginia

1963: Herschel Gibson dies in a car accident at age 30

1960s: Wilma's childhood in Appalachia

1968: Wilma forms the first country and western band at age 12

Early 1970s: Wilma drops out in 11th grade

Mid 1970s: Earns GED, attends four-year college

Late 1970s: Begins teaching career, language arts to 7th-8th graders

1980s-1990s: Continues music career with multiple bands

Mid 1980s: I went to college and started teaching that year

1991: Ruby Gibson (Mama) passes away

2006: Eckle Gibson (Daddy) passes away on Christmas Day

2006-2009: Three years of severe depression following Daddy's death

2017: Retires from 31 years of teaching

2017: Begins cattle farming with husband in Lawrenceburg, Tennessee

2026: Writes memoir at age 70

About the Author

Wilma Gibson Smith was born in 1956 in Kemmergem, Virginia, the youngest of ten children in a coal-mining family. Despite leaving school in the eleventh grade, she later earned her GED, completed her college degree, and spent thirty-three years shaping young minds as a Language Arts teacher for seventh and eighth graders.

A lifelong musician, Wilma formed her first country and western band at the age of twelve. She performed throughout the region for over twenty years and even recorded a record with her final band. Today, music remains a cornerstone of her life; she continues to play the piano, sing, and enjoy making music with her husband and grandchildren.

Following her retirement from teaching, Wilma and her husband transitioned to cattle farming in Lawrenceburg, Tennessee, where they have worked side-by-side for the past eight years. Her favorite part of farming is the arrival of new calves; a constant reminder that new beginnings are always possible.

Wilma has one son and two grandchildren. At seventy, she continues to live by the values her parents instilled in her: faith in God, devotion to family, the dignity of honest work, and the unwavering belief that where you start doesn't determine where you are going.

Forged in the Mountains: A Family's Resilience is her first book.